creatures
of the sea

Sea
Horses

Other titles in the series:

creatures of the sea

Sea Horses

Kris Hirschmann

KIDHAVEN PRESS

An imprint of Thomson Gale, a part of The Thomson Corporation

THOMSON ™

GALE

San Diego • Detroit • New York • San Francisco • Cleveland
New Haven, Conn. • Waterville, Maine • London • Munich

© 2005 Thomson Gale, a part of The Thomson Corporation.

Thomson and Star Logo are trademarks and Gale and KidHaven Press are registered trademarks used herein under license.

For more information, contact
KidHaven Press
27500 Drake Rd.
Farmington Hills, MI 48331-3535
Or you can visit our Internet site at http://www.gale.com

LIBRARY OF CONGRESS CATALOGING-IN-PUBLICATION DATA

Hirschmann, Kris, 1967–
   Sea horses / by Kris Hirschmann.
     p. cm. — (Creatures of the sea)
   Includes bibliographical references (p.   ).
   ISBN 0-7377-2344-0 (hardback : alk. paper)
Summary: Discusses the habitats, anatomy, mating habits, and hunting methods of sea horses. Also discusses threat posed by humans as well as conservation efforts.
   1. Sea horses—Juvenile literature. I. Title.

Printed in the United States of America

Table of Contents

Myth and Reality

People have always been fascinated by sea horses. These ocean animals inspired many myths and legends during long-ago times. In Greek mythology, the sea god Poseidon traveled in a chariot pulled by sea horses. The Romans had a similar myth in which sea horses were the favorite animals of Neptune, the king of the sea. Waves crashing along the shore were supposedly created by sea horses pulling King Neptune's chariot.

Chinese legends also linked sea horses with sea gods. One traditional Chinese story tells of a sea god who had to reach the other side of the earth but did not know how to get there. After some thought, the god decided to bring horses into the ocean to pull his carriage. But when the horses were brought underwater, they started to drown. Quickly the god used his magic to make the horses breathe water instead of air, thus creating the world's first sea horses.

It is not surprising that legends associated sea horses with the land variety. The sea horse's head does look a little like that of a horse. In fact, the sea horse's scientific name, **Hippocampus**, comes from Greek words meaning horse (*hippos*) and monster (*campus*). The "horse" part of the name comes from the sea horse's head, and the "monster" part probably comes from this animal's unusual shape.

Because of their unusual shape, sea horses have inspired legends and myths for thousands of years.

This name is a bit misleading. Sea horses are not related to horses, and they certainly are not monsters. They also are not legends. Sea horses are real living creatures that can be found all over the world. In the wild, most sea horses are very hard to spot. But they are there, and any careful observer can find them if he or she looks hard enough. Every day people around the globe catch glimpses of these living legends.

Armored Fish

I dentifying sea horse **species** is a confusing task. At one time, scientists believed there were more than 120 different sea horse species. They did not realize that sea horses of the same species may look very different. These differences fooled early scientists into thinking they were discovering new species. Sometimes ten or more scientific names were given to the same type of sea horse.

Modern researchers are working to correct these mistakes. Scientists today recognize thirty to thirty-five sea horse species. All of these species belong to the genus *Hippocampus* and the family **Sygnathidae**, which also includes pipefishes, pipe horses, and sea dragons. Despite their strange looks, all of these animals are fish. Scientists include sea horses and their relatives in the fish family because they breathe with gills and swim with fins.

Finding Sea Horses

Sea horses are saltwater animals. They live in tropical and temperate (cool but not cold) ocean waters. Most species prefer shallow coastal waters no deeper than fifty feet (15.2 m). Some species, such as the short-nosed sea horse and the pot-bellied sea horse, may be found in slightly deeper waters (one hundred feet (30.4 m) or more). A few species are even **pelagic**, which means they live in the open ocean. Pelagic sea horses probably make their homes in floating beds of seaweed.

Sea horses are found just about anywhere the water is warm enough. These creatures live along the coasts of every continent except Antarctica. Several species live in the Mediterranean and Red seas. Sea horses are especially common in the Indo-Pacific region, where the Indian and Pacific oceans come together. This area includes Indonesia, the Philippines, Papua New Guinea, northeastern Australia, and the many island nations of the western Pacific Ocean. Sea horses are also common in the western Atlantic region, which includes the eastern coasts of the United States and Central America as well as the Caribbean and the Gulf of Mexico.

The best places to look for sea horses include coral reefs and sea grass beds. Sea horses may also live near mangrove trees, whose root systems grow into the water. All of these habitats give the sea horse lots of places to hide. They also provide plenty of slender branches and stalks to which the sea horse can cling. Any object to which a sea horse clings is called a **holdfast**.

With the exception of the pelagic species, sea horses have very small home ranges. Male sea

Scuba divers can find sea horses in coral reefs, beds of sea grass, or other habitats.

horses do not travel more than a couple of feet from their holdfasts. In fact, many choose a favorite holdfast and use it as long as they live. Females have a much larger range, about a hundred times that of the males.

Sizes and Shapes

Sea horses come in many different sizes. The smallest species is the pygmy sea horse, which measures less than one inch (2.54 cm) when fully grown. The largest species is the big-bellied sea horse, which can grow to more than one foot (30.48 cm) in length. Sea horses are measured from the top of the head to the tip of the tail. However, sea horses almost always keep their tails tightly curled. For this reason, sea horses usually look smaller than their "official" length.

No matter what their size, all sea horses are built the same way. At the top of the sea horse's body is the horselike head that gives this animal its nickname. The most noticeable features on the head are the long, tube-shaped snout and two knobby eyes, one on each side of the head. The top of the head is formed into a bony bump called the **coronet**. Tiny differences in the shape and size of the coronet can be used to tell one sea horse from another. Some scientists say sea horses' coronets are as different as human fingerprints.

Starting behind the head, the sea horse's body is divided into a series of bony rings. These rings are

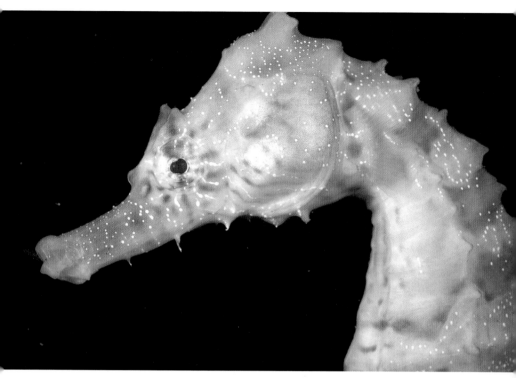

The coronet is the bony bump at the top of the sea horse's head. The bump's shape is different from one sea horse to another.

the sea horse's substitute for the hard scales found on most fish. They are covered with a layer of skin. In some species the skin is padded so the rings cannot be seen. In many species, however, the skin is stretched so tightly that the ridges between the rings are easy to spot. The number of rings varies from species to species but is usually between forty-five and fifty.

The widest rings are found in the trunk area, which starts just below the sea horse's neck. The trunk is narrow at the top but quickly widens into a bulging belly.

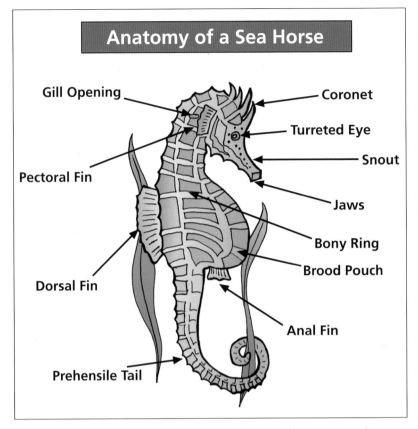

Anatomy of a Sea Horse

Gill Opening
Coronet
Turreted Eye
Snout
Pectoral Fin
Jaws
Bony Ring
Brood Pouch
Dorsal Fin
Anal Fin
Prehensile Tail

The rings of the trunk surround and protect the sea horse's most important internal organs.

Below the trunk, the sea horse's body narrows into a slender tail. There are about three times as many rings in the tail as there are in the trunk. The tail is **prehensile**, which means it can curl. The sea horse uses its prehensile tail to cling to its holdfast, other sea horses, or anything else it wants to grasp.

Identifying Sea Horses

There are many differences between sea horse species and sexes. The easiest difference to spot is the presence or absence of a **brood pouch**. This is a rounded, fleshy area starting just below the trunk and continuing partway down the tail. Only male sea horses have a brood pouch. In females, the last ring of the trunk juts out sharply from the tail with no brood pouch to soften the change.

Another difference between sea horses is their size and shape. Height, width, and nose length can all be used to tell species apart. Some species' scientific names were even chosen because of these differences. *Hippocampus abdominalis,* for instance, means "big-bellied sea horse," and *Hippocampus brevirostris* means "short-nosed sea horse."

Several other features besides size and shape can help identify sea horse species. For instance, different sea horses have different numbers of bony rings in the trunk, tail, or both. The shape of the coronet varies from species to species. And spines on the sea horse's snout, cheeks, and forehead have unique shapes. All of these features provide important clues to a sea horse's identity.

Changing Features

Sometimes skin color can be used to identify sea horses. Some sea horses are even named for their special colors. The zebra sea horse, for example, gets its name from the black-and-white stripes on its body, and the lined sea horse often has blotchy patches on the black-and-white lines on its neck.

Color, however, is not usually a good way to identify sea horses. These animals can change their skin color at will, so the same sea horse may look very different from one day to the next.

Skin filaments are the last feature sometimes used to identify sea horses. Filaments are fleshy strings or knobs sticking out from the sea horse's body. Like skin color, however, the filaments are not fixed. A sea horse can change them to match its surroundings. So filaments are not the best way to tell sea horses apart.

Getting Around

One thing that makes sea horses different from other fish is their upright posture. Most fish have their heads at the front of the body and their tails at the rear, but sea horses have their heads at the top of the body and their tails at the bottom. They keep this position even when they are swimming.

Most fish use their tails to swim. Sea horses, however, do not use their tails for this purpose. Instead they use a small fin on their backs. The sea horse's swimming fin is called the **dorsal fin**. The dorsal fin contains many spines that are connected by a transparent web. The spines move independently, pulling the web back and forth very quickly in a pattern that looks like a wave. This wave is called an **undulation**. The undulating dorsal fin disturbs the water and pushes the sea horse forward.

Lined sea horses sometimes have blotchy patches on the black-and-white lines on their necks.

The sea horse also uses two **pectoral fins** to help it swim. The pectoral fins are found at the back of the sea horse's head, one on each side. They work much like the dorsal fin. But instead of providing a forward push, the pectoral fins create a sideways push. This lets the sea horse turn its body to the

A long-nosed sea horse uses the small fin on its back to move through a bed of sea grass.

right or the left as it moves through the water. The pectoral fins also help with balance and stability.

The **air bladder** is the sea horse's last swimming tool. The sea horse uses this organ to hold or release gas. When the air bladder is full of gas, the sea horse becomes **buoyant** and rises like a balloon. When the air bladder is empty, the sea horse is heavier than the water around it, and it sinks. By filling and emptying the air bladder, the sea horse moves up and down whenever it likes.

Sea horses are not fast swimmers. It would take an average sea horse about five minutes to cross a bathtub full of water. But what these creatures lack in speed, they make up in accuracy. Sea horses usually live in tangles of grass, coral branches, and other obstacle-rich areas. Slow, delicate movement is just what the sea horse needs to get around in its underwater home.

chapter 2

Family Matters

No one is sure how long sea horses live in the wild. In aquariums, sea horses live between one and five years, depending on their size. Small sea horses have the shortest life spans, while larger sea horses usually live longer.

During their short lifetimes, sea horses put a great deal of time and energy into creating babies. These animals have a very unusual way of reproducing. The males, not the females, become pregnant and give birth. Pipefish, which are close relatives of the sea horse, are the only other animals that reproduce in this way.

The Mating Process

Sea horses breed during the warmest months of the year. This period is known as the breeding season. Sea horses usually stay with the same mate throughout a breeding season. Sometimes they even mate for life.

Male sea horses start the breeding process by "dancing" with their mates. A dancing male may swim in circles around the female or wrap his tail around her body. He may change his skin color to show the female he is ready to mate. He also opens his brood pouch again and again. Scientists think this action is meant to show the female that the brood pouch is empty and ready to be filled with eggs.

If the female likes what she sees, she stays near the dancing male. She watches him carefully. Soon she begins nodding her head up and down. Then she starts to create a batch of ripe eggs inside her body.

A male sea horse wraps his tail around a female to show her that he is ready to mate.

The number of eggs varies from species to species. The smallest sea horses may produce just five eggs at a time. Larger species may produce more than fifteen hundred eggs at once. The entire process takes as much as three days from beginning to end.

By the time the eggs are ready, the female's belly bulges outward. The ripe eggs are large and heavy. Together, they may equal about one-third of the female's body weight. Creating such a large egg mass takes a lot of energy—and if the eggs are not used right away, they will die. This is probably why female sea horses wait for their mates to dance before they start working on a batch of eggs. By making sure the males are ready to breed, the females do not waste their strength by creating useless eggs.

A final courtship dance begins after the female's eggs are ready. This dance may last as long as nine hours. Finally the male and female sea horses press their bellies together. The female uses a fleshy tube called an **ovipositor** to squirt her eggs into the male's brood pouch. The sea horses make clicking sounds as they mate by tossing their heads up and down.

A Short Pregnancy

The male and female separate as soon as all the eggs are laid. The male's brood pouch seals shut. Inside the pouch, the eggs are fertilized by the male's sperm. The fertilized eggs settle into the pouch lining and start to develop.

A male with a full brood pouch clings to a blade of sea grass.

Scientists have learned that a male sea horse's brood pouch works just like the womb of any female animal. Blood vessels in the walls of the pouch carry oxygen to the developing eggs and remove waste products. Liquids inside the pouch are carefully balanced to provide the best possible environment for the eggs. The pregnant sea horse even makes a special chemical called **prolactin** that maintains the brood pouch during pregnancy. This is the same chemical that helps human females make milk after they give birth.

The male's pregnancy lasts between ten days and six weeks, depending on the species and the water temperature. (The warmer the water, the shorter the pregnancy.) The male and the female do not stay together throughout this time. However, the female does swim over to see her mate each morning during his pregnancy. Some scientists call this visit the "morning greeting." During the morning greeting, the sea horses wrap their tails around each other. They may take a short swim around the male's territory. Often they change colors as if to show each other that they are glad to be together.

The morning greeting does not last long. The female stays for only five to ten minutes before releasing her mate and swimming away. The male then goes back to his holdfast. The female will stay away until the next morning, when she will return once again to greet her mate.

A female sea horse (right) greets her pregnant mate.

Scientists believe that the morning greeting is more than just a way to say "hello." They think it is also a way for sea horses to coordinate their mating cycles. Because the female sees the male every day, she knows right away when he has given birth, and she can start working on a new batch of eggs immediately. In this way very little time is wasted between one pregnancy and the next.

Babies Are Born

Toward the end of a pregnancy, the environment inside the male's brood pouch changes. The liquid surrounding the eggs becomes more and more like seawater. Around the time this change happens, the eggs hatch inside the brood pouch. The little sea horses remain inside the pouch, getting bigger and stronger.

Finally the father is ready to eject his babies into the open sea. The muscles of the brood pouch start to tighten as the male goes into labor. The sea horse clings to his holdfast and begins jerking his body back and forth. With each jerk the brood pouch opens, and the babies (sometimes called **ponies**) start to appear. Some species eject just one pony with each jerk. Others send out a stream of tiny sea horses each time their pouch pops open. Depending on the number of babies in the brood pouch, the birth process can take anywhere from a few minutes to a day or even more. It usually happens during the night.

The newborn sea horses look just like adults, but they are much smaller. The little creatures measure between one-eighth and one-half inch (.318 and 1.27 cm), depending on their species. As soon as they hit the water, the ponies drift away to begin their life in the sea. They will not see their father again, and they will never meet their mother.

As soon as all his babies are gone, a male sea horse gets ready to mate again. He greets his mate with a courtship dance when she appears the next morning. In response, the female starts working on a new batch of eggs, and breeding takes place soon afterward. The male becomes pregnant again just a few days after giving birth.

Adult sea horses repeat their breeding cycle many times throughout the warm season. Scientists have not studied all species of sea horses to see how many pregnancies they have. One Australian species, however, is known to have about seven broods per year. Depending on the length of the pregnancy and the temperature of the water, other species probably have a few more or less pregnancies than this.

Growing Up

While the sea horse parents continue the breeding cycle, the ponies struggle to survive on their own. Some newborn sea horses manage to grab a holdfast near the ocean floor and stay there as they grow. Others

An Australian sea horse ejects his babies into the open sea.

A close-up shows that ponies look like tiny adult sea horses.

are swept away by ocean currents. Even the smallest sea horses can swim freely if they find themselves in open water. If possible, however, a drifting pony clings to twigs, seaweed, or other scraps of floating material. It may even wrap its tiny tail around another pony if it cannot find anything else to hold.

Wherever a pony ends up, its first job is to find food. Newborn sea horses must eat constantly to survive. They hunt for even tinier creatures, sucking them into their tubelike snouts. Successful hunters grow quickly. Before long, a sea horse is big enough and strong enough to make its way to the ocean floor. Once there, it finds a comfortable holdfast and settles into an adult lifestyle. After a few months the young sea horse is ready to find a mate and produce babies of its own.

Very few sea horses, however, will make it to this stage. Nearly all ponies are eaten by larger animals within days of their birth. In fact, some scientists estimate that throughout their entire lives, a breeding pair will produce only two babies that survive to adulthood. This is a very low survival rate—but it is enough. As long as sea horses keep mating and releasing new ponies into the ocean, populations of these amazing animals will continue to thrive.

Feeding and Hiding

Sea horses are **predators**. This means they hunt and eat living animals to survive. Sea horses eat mostly brine shrimp, which are tiny swimming crustaceans (animals with external skeletons, such as shrimp and crabs) less than one-quarter inch (.635 cm) long. However, they will eat just about anything that fits into their mouths. Newly hatched fish and the **larvae** (small, immature forms) of many different sea creatures make good meals for a hungry sea horse.

Sea horses are not just hunters. They are also hunted by other animals. Because sea horses swim so slowly, they cannot escape easily from fish and other fast-moving creatures. Therefore they stay hidden to keep themselves safe. Indeed, sea horses are among the ocean's best-hidden creatures.

Hungry Predators

Almost all sea horses are daytime hunters. They hunt when it is light out because they depend on their eyes to help them find food. A sea horse can move its bulging eyes separately. By shifting its eyes in different directions, the sea horse can look to both sides at the same time. By pointing both of its eyes forward, the sea horse can look straight ahead. Having the ability to look wherever it likes helps the sea horse to spot prey. Looking forward with both eyes at once also helps the sea horse to focus on any prey, no matter how tiny.

With its tail wrapped around a blade of sea grass, a hungry dwarf sea horse waits for drifting prey.

All sea horses use a sit-and-wait hunting method. With its tail wrapped around a holdfast, a sea horse looks for drifting prey. Before long, the sea horse will probably spot a brine shrimp or another tasty meal. The sea horse beats its fins to shift its body into position. It moves slowly and carefully so it will not scare away its prey. The sea horse tries to get the tip of its snout within about an inch (2.54 cm) of its intended meal.

When the sea horse gets close enough, it prepares to strike. It opens the tip of its snout, which is hinged like a trap door. The sea horse then uses muscles in its head to pull down on bony plates that line the mouth floor. The plates drop very quickly, creating a powerful suction. It takes only a fraction of a second for prey to be slurped into the sea horse's mouth. Once inside, the unlucky animal is swallowed whole by the hungry predator.

Messy Eaters

Sea horses are messy eaters. Immediately after a sea horse swallows, a cloud of food particles floats out of its gill slits (found on the sides of the head). The animal's head seems to smoke as food passes into its system. This smoky effect lasts for just a moment. The sea horse's meal quickly moves into the throat and then, since sea horses have no stomachs, directly into the intestine. The food is digested on its way through the intestine.

Because they lack stomachs, sea horses cannot store food inside their bodies for long. For this reason their digestive systems are very inefficient. As a result, sea horses do not get as much nutrition from a meal as other animals do. They make up for their fast digestion by eating constantly. A big sea horse might eat nearly four thousand brine shrimp in a single day. If a sea horse goes without food for even a few hours, it may die of starvation.

Masters of Disguise

Even when they are hunting, sea horses do their best to stay hidden. If they do not keep out of sight, they risk becoming meals for other animals. Larger

To hide from other animals, a long-nosed sea horse changes its skin color and blends into its background.

fish, crabs, skates, rays, and even penguins eat sea horses. One sea horse was even found in the stomach of a sea turtle.

Sea horses use many different types of **camouflage** to keep themselves safe. Camouflage means that the sea horse blends into its background and becomes very hard to see. The most important way it does this

A pygmy sea horse with pink skin and wartlike bumps all over its body looks like a piece of coral.

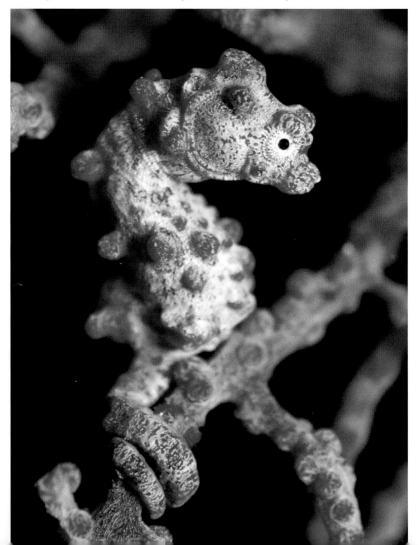

is by changing its skin color. Sea horses can change their color at will to match the coral, rocks, or grass of their home area. They do this with special skin cells called **chromatophores**. Chromatophores come in many different colors, and each one is controlled by tiny muscles. When the muscles are relaxed, the chromatophores are small and do not show much of their color. But when the muscles contract, the chromatophores are pulled open. Their color suddenly shows up much more clearly. Sea horses open and close different patterns of chromatophores to adjust their body colors as needed.

A Perfect Match

Sea horses can also grow fleshy filaments on their bodies to hide themselves. The shape and size of the filaments matches the sea horse's home. The pygmy sea horse, for example, grows wartlike bumps all over its body to match the lumpy coral in which it lives. Then it adjusts the color of these bumps so they look exactly like the coral. And the White's sea horse grows thin, waving filaments that blend with the kelp and sea grass of this animal's home.

Sometimes sea horses let sand or other particles settle on their skin. They may even let algae grow on their bodies. Covered by these substances, a sea horse blends so well into its surroundings that it is almost impossible to see.

The best camouflage in the world, of course, would not keep a sea horse hidden if it was quickly darting from place to place. Predators would be sure to notice any fast movements. The sea horse's calm lifestyle is therefore another defense against hungry animals. Usually a sea horse stays in one place, tightly grasping a secure holdfast. It does not move or draw attention to itself. And even if a sea horse must move from one place to another, it travels so slowly that it looks like a drifting scrap of wood or seaweed. Unless another animal nearly bumps into the sea horse, it probably will not even notice this slow-moving creature.

The only part of the sea horse's body that moves quickly is the dorsal fin. But even this motion is no problem. For one thing, the dorsal fin is transparent (see-through). Also, the dorsal fin beats more than twenty times per second. This movement is so fast that it cannot be seen by fish and other predators, whose eyes are designed to track much slower motions.

Many Uses

Camouflage and slow movement cannot always save the sea horse from humans. People pull these animals from the ocean, then sell them. Some scientists estimate that between 20 and 24 million sea horses are traded each year around the world.

Why are sea horses so popular? It is because people have found many uses for these bony creatures.

Strings of dried sea horses hang in a shop in Vietnam.

In some Asian countries, especially China, Taiwan, Hong Kong, and Singapore, sea horses are the main ingredient in many popular medicines. Powdered sea horse is said to cure health problems, including asthma, dizziness, poor appetite, and more. There is no scientific evidence that these claims are true. But people have been putting their faith in sea horse-based powders for hundreds of years, and they are not about to stop now. They keep buying traditional medicines, so suppliers keep taking these animals from the sea.

Sea horses are also sold as souvenirs in many areas. Tourists who visit seaside vacation spots snap up sea horse key chains, wall hangings, and other knickknacks. To create these objects, people tie threads around the necks of living sea horses. Then they hang the sea horses in the hot sun until they die and their bodies dry out.

In Captivity

In the United States, sea horses are not usually made into medicine or souvenirs. They are, however, sold live to aquarium owners. In one way this use is better than the others, because the sea horses are not killed before they are sold. But unfortunately, most aquarium sea horses die before long. Sea horses are so picky about their food that they are hard to keep in captivity. Very few aquarium owners have the knowledge or the patience they need to raise sea horses away from their home environment.

World Populations

No one knows how many sea horses there are in the world, and no one knows whether populations are being hurt by fishing industries. But scientists are worried. They think the current yearly harvest is too large, and they are urging people everywhere to be more careful. These scientists are starting to get results. For instance, all sea horse species are now listed on the International Union for the Conservation of Nature (IUCN) Red List. The Red List warns the world that a species is at risk of becoming endangered.

A sea horse fisherman in the Philippines shows some of his catch.

Individuals are also taking action. In the Philippines, for example, some sea horse fishers do not sell young sea horses right away. They put them into "grow-out cages" for several months. During this time, male sea horses usually give birth to several batches of ponies.

In other areas, fishing villages are setting up marine **sanctuaries** to protect sea horses. Animals grow freely inside the sanctuaries without fear of being harmed. Before long, populations begin to spread outside the sanctuaries and into commercial fishing areas. People can find and catch plenty of sea horses without disturbing their core breeding stock.

Simple actions like these are important because they help the ocean sea horse population to maintain itself. With just a little care, these unusual fish will be swimming the world's seas for countless years to come.

Glossary

air bladder: An organ that can hold or release gas.

brood pouch: A sac on the belly of a male sea horse in which eggs develop and hatch.

buoyant: Able to float.

camouflage: Skin coloring designed to blend into the background.

chromatophores: Color cells in the skin that can get bigger or smaller, thereby changing a sea horse's color.

coronet: A bony "crown" on top of a sea horse's head.

dorsal fin: The transparent fin on a sea horse's back.

filaments: Fleshy knobs or strings growing on the sea horse's body.

Hippocampus: The genus name for all sea horses.

holdfast: Any object to which a sea horse clings.

larvae: The name for many newly hatched creatures before they change into their adult form.

ovipositor: A fleshy tube a female sea horse uses to deposit her eggs.

pectoral fins: Two transparent fins, one on each side of the sea horse's head.

pelagic: Living in the open ocean.

ponies: A name sometimes given to young sea horses.

predator: Any animal that hunts other animals.

prehensile: Able to curl.

prolactin: A chemical produced by the male sea horse during pregnancy.

sanctuaries: Protected places where wildlife cannot be hunted.

species: A distinct type of animal. The bottom level of the scientific classification system.

Sygnathidae: The scientific family that includes sea horses and their closest relatives.

undulation: A wavelike back-and-forth motion.

For Further Exploration

Books and Magazines

Frank Indiviglio, *Seahorses: Everything About History, Care, Nutrition, Handling, and Behavior.* Hauppage, NY: Barron's, 2002. A must-read book for anyone hoping to keep sea horses in a home aquarium.

Sara Swan Miller, *Seahorses, Pipefishes, and Their Kin.* New York: Franklin Watts, 2002. This book explores the classification of sea horses. It also gives profiles of fifteen members of the Sygnathidae family, including several sea horses.

Amanda Vincent, "The Improbable Seahorse," *National Geographic,* October 1994. Written by the world's main sea horse scientist, this article has a lot of good background information and pictures. It also discusses the uses of sea horses around the world.

Web Sites

Kingdom of the Seahorse (www.pbs.org/wgbh/nova/seahorse). This is a companion site to the NOVA TV program "Kingdom of the Seahorse," first broadcast in April 1997. It includes lots of pictures plus a section on sea horse anatomy and a good interview with sea horse scientist Amanda Vincent.

Project Seahorse (http://seahorse.fisheries.ubc.ca). Read about sea horse anatomy, habitat, classification, life span, and reproduction.

Seahorse (http://users.ipfw.edu/mustafaa/seahorse.ppt). This slide show includes profiles and pictures of twelve sea horse species.

index

picture credits

Cover image: Photos.com
AP/Wide World Photos, 24
Gregory G. Dimijian/Photo Researchers, Inc.,
    13, 18, 23, 31
© Reinhard Dirscherl/Visuals Unlimited, 7, 34
© Owen Franken/CORBIS, 37
© Stephen Frink/CORBIS, 11
Robb Kendrick/Aurora, 39
© Ken Lucas/Visuals Unlimited, 17
Suzanne Santillan, 14
VVG/Photo Researchers, Inc., 28
© Lawson Wood/CORBIS, 33
© Norbert Wu/Minden Pictures, 21
Paul A. Zahl/Photo Researchers, Inc., 27

about the author

Kris Hirschmann has written more than one hundred books for children. She is the president of The Wordshop, a business that provides a variety of writing and editorial services. She holds a bachelor's degree in psychology from Dartmouth College in Hanover, New Hampshire.

Hirschmann lives just outside Orlando, Florida, with her husband, Michael, and her daughters, Nikki and Erika.